Turtle Care : A Guide From A Veterinarian On Caring For Your Turtle

Make Your Turtle Live For 50 Years Or More

By: Donald Wilson

TABLE OF CONTENTS

Publishers Notes

BINDERS PUBLISHING LLC

7950 NW 53rd Street

Miami,

FL 33166

Kindle Edition 2012

BINDERS PUBLISHING PRESS is a trademark of Binders Publishing LLC.

For information about special discounts for bulk purchases, please contact Binders Publishing Sales Department at 646-312-7900 or publishing@binderspublishing.com

Designed by Colin WF Scott

Manufactured in the United States of America

DEDICATION

I want to dedicate this book to everyone that loves turtles, especially my mother that gave me my first pet turtle. Thanks MOM!

CHAPTER 1- WHAT YOU NEED TO KNOW ABOUT TURTLE BEFORE YOU BUY THEM

It is very crucial that before you actually purchase a turtle that you get all the information you possibly can before you bring a turtle home. It is will be necessary for you to find out what it takes to be a turtle owner; how much it costs and the kind of time you will need to invest to have a turtle as a pet. Learn about the special care that they need, their health issues, the fact that if they do not receive the special care that they need then they lead a life that is of poor quality and their life expectancy will be cut short.

Where they will live, what they eat; basically what makes them happy and healthy, who will take care of them when you have to go on a business trip or vacation, and will you have the time every day to take care of them are among the things that you need to learn prior to getting a turtle as a pet. In addition, you should also settle in your own mind as to why you want a turtle and if that decision is based on you loving the creatures and wanting to take care of them, then you should go for it.

Other specific factors that you have to take into consideration before buying a turtle is that owning a turtle will cost you hundreds of dollars in bedding, temperature, food, vitamins, vet care etc. This is important to note since turtles tend to live for very long; twenty five years or more.

In addition, you have to give them clean food, water and bedding every day, which means that you are expected to spend at least thirty minutes every day with your turtle. Since turtles do hibernate for ten and twenty weeks, you will need to create the appropriate environment for them to do so. They are also prone to certain diseases such as salmonella and they have a tendency to bite. Finally, you should also research the different species of turtles so that you can make an informed decision when you finally decide that you definitely want to have a turtle as a pet.

CHAPTER 2- BEST TYPE OF PET TURTLE TO BUY : DIFFERENT SPECIES AND WHICH ONE MAKES THE BEST PET

The decision to purchase a turtle as a pet is a very important one. Now that the decision is made you will need to find out the different types of turtles that are recommended as pets and then figure out which one you want to take home with you. The turtles that make the best pets are Red Eared Sliders, Box Turtles (Eastern Box Turtle), Western Painted Turtle, Map Turtle, Wood Turtle, and the Mud Turtle.

The Red Eared Sliders, although they are sold in pet stores as young turtles, they usually grow to a foot long and therefore by the time they get to be adults they will need a very large aquarium of about one hundred gallons. They are small in size and quite pretty. They are the most popular pet turtle in the United States as well as in a number of other countries.

These turtles are native to the southern areas of the United States and there name is derived from a unique red patch of skin that is around their ears. The slider in their name is derived from their being able to slide from logs and rocks and quickly get into the water. They are mostly aquatic but they will leave the water to lay their eggs and to lie in the sun. They must eat their food in water as they a have fixed tongue so they do not produce saliva.

The box turtle is also a very good choice for a pet turtle. These are native to North America; specifically to Mexico and the United States. It is characterized mostly by its domed shell that is hinged underneath, enabling the turtle to tightly close its shell in its attempt to get away from its predators. Although, this is a species that is popular as a pet, it does have complex needs when they are in captivity.

The Eastern Box Turtle is also found in in the United States and Mexico, may be the most popular of all the Box Turtles as pets. They live near ponds and streams in grasslands and in marshes and woodlands. They thrive much better in between seventy five and eighty degrees of temperature. If they are kept on the inside, then their owners will need to install a full spectrum of ultraviolet lighting.

One of the most beautiful of the turtle family is the Painted Turtle. Their marking and shells are very beautiful. These turtles spend most of their lives in water and as such, they should be kept in a tank preferably. Even though they spend most of the time in their tank, the Painted Turtle will still need to have an area set up for them to bask in the sun and hey will need the usual in which to do so; a heat lamp, UV light and an appropriate place in which to bask.

With the Western Painted Turtles, the adult will grow to between seven and eight inches. This species of turtle is found in Canada and the United States. They prefer to live in river flood plains, river oxbows and in prairie wetlands. In captive, and living on the outside, they should be kept in a fifty to a one hundred and fifty gallon pond and if they are being housed indoors, then a small tank of twenty gallons is what is recommended. They need a platform such as a log, a rock or a basking platform that you can find in a pet store, as they need to bask. They will also need a basking light that will provide them with ultraviolet rays as well as a heating lamp that is about ninety degrees, and water temperature that is approximately seventy degrees.

The females of the Map Turtle species measure between six and ten inches as adults. The males are half as big as they are. They too are found in Canada and in the United States. In the wild they live in moving waters like large streams and rivers, while in captivity they need warm climate and a large tank; forty gallon or more. If you live in a climate that is warm they can live outside all year round. However, whether they live inside or outdoors they will need sites to bask in but if they live inside, then they will need an ultraviolet lamp that gives off temperatures of between eighty four and ninety four degrees and their water temperature should be between seventy two and eighty degrees.

The Wood Turtle grows to between five and nine inches. They are natives of the United States and Canada and in the wild they live near streams, lakes and rivers. In captivity they need an enclosure that is at least five feet long and five feet wide and should have a place from which they can draw themselves out of so that they can bask under a heat lam an a ultraviolet light. Their basking spot should be approximately eighty five degrees in temperature and a water temperature of between sixty and seventy degrees.

CHAPTER 3- CREATING THE RIGHT ENVIRONMENT FOR YOUR TURTLE : PROVIDING A GOOD HABITAT

Proper housing for your turtle is not just about having somewhere for them to live, but also involves keeping them healthy, as their habitat can make them sick if it does not have the correct lighting, humidity and temperatures that they need to survive in captivity. Their habitat should be cleaned regularly and they should be provided with a sturdy bowl for water; sturdy so that they will not be able to push it over and leave them without water for any extended periods.

Box turtles may be one of the easiest turtles to house since their needs are fewer than most other species. However, they do not like confinement and prefer the outdoors. They are in need of a lot of space, so an outside pen of about four feet by four feet should be more than sufficient as a habitat for them. A simple frame with walls of approximately two feet off the ground; extended for about one foot under the ground is a good dimension as they are very good diggers and anything less than this could allow them to dig their way out of the enclosure. Although a cover for an outside enclosure is optional, it may be used as a means of security if the pen is being threatened by either dogs or raccoons, as these animals can be dangerous to them. If you are not able to house them outside however, a big aquarium should comfortably house them indoors. For a Red-Eared Slider, a 20, 30 or 55 gallon aquarium would be sufficient space to house them; dependent on the number of turtles you are housing in one tank as well as the sizes of your turtles. If they are being kept in a tank lighting is crucial as they will be dependent on full-spectrum lighting; an artificial type of lighting that is a replica of the sun's energy to keep them healthy.

You can add natural plants such as perennials to a turtles habitat is a very good idea. You can create hide areas by using large rocks that you should cement together. Turtles also need to bask, and as such, it is necessary that you have the proper fluorescent lighting to provide them with what they need to keep their vitamin levels at the right balance.

CHAPTER 4- WHAT TO FEED YOUR PET TURTLE TO MAKE LIVE LONGER : THE BEST FOOD AND SCHEDULES TO FEED YOUR TURTLE

The frequency with which your turtle is being fed and how much he is fed at each feeding will be partially dependent on their age. When they are living in the wild, some turtles will eat snails, crayfish, insects and plants, while others will eat almost anything except for aquatic, soft vegetation and do not eat as much as their counterparts. The onus is on the owner to make sure they observe their pet turtle so that they will see the amount of food they need so that they will maintain their health but not too much that will sicken them or cause them to gain too much wait.

The day time is time of the day in which the Red eared Sliders are their most active. As such, this is the time during which they should be fed. A number of turtle owners usually feed their Red Eared Sliders every day. Those Red Eared Turtles who are in captive usually eat aquatic turtle foods but some owners feed them live foods which are sometimes supplemented by packaged food. They are fed with crickets, raw fish, mealworms and heartworms. They are herbivorous when they are in the wild and as such, they can also have cucumbers, cabbage, carrots, beets, lettuce among other vegetables in their diet as well.

One of the pickiest eaters in the turtle family is the Box Turtle. The problem with box turtles is that if they are not happy with where they live in captivity they will just stop eating completely, they are that temperamental. Even if they are comfortable in captivity, they are still partial to the types of foods they do accept so you just have to keep trying them with different foods if you know their habitat is comfortable but they still will not eat. The good news is that they do eat a wide variety of foods when they do eat such as earthworms, flies, spiders, crickets and grasshoppers. They are mostly herbivorous however and therefore they will also eat different types of vegetables and fruits. They like strawberries, carrots, apples, bananas, cantelopes, beets and cucumbers. You can make them fruits salads and store it in the refrigerators and then giving them a spoonful from time to time.

The Western Painted Turtles usually eat insects, small fishes, worms, duckweed, crayfish, snails, tadpoles, leeches and frogs. They also eat carrots, earthworms, lettuce, crickets, turtle food from pet store, waxworms, some plants, aquatic snails, bananas, squash, berries, apples, green beans, dandelions etc.

Map Turtle will eat both vegetation and meat. As such, they can be fed different kinds of food such as waxworms, leafy green vegetables, mealworms fish, crickets, earthworms, carrots and commercially prepared turtle food. They should be fed daily when they are young and every other day when they become adults. You should also supplement their foods with multi-vitamin and calcium.

Wood Turtles usually eat live worms, crickets, pinky mice, plant matter such as strawberries, wild violets, cinquefoil, greenbrier, mullein, sorrel, plantain, cranberry leaves and dandelions mosses and mushrooms and they will eat corn right off the cob. They also like animal matter such as earthworm, slugs, leeches and snails.

Mud Turtles are omnivores so they do eat plants as well as animals. They prefer to eat such things like fish, insects, tadpoles, algae, and carrots.

Chapter 5- How To Monitor The Health Of Your Turtle : Common Health Issues And How To Treat Them

Salmonellosis and Soft Shell are conditions that are common to the turtle family. Salmonellosis is an infection of the intestine which the turtles usually get from other turtles that are infected and passed on to human beings through bacteria that is picked up from surroundings that are unclean like feces and dirty water.

You can help your turtles not to be infected by salmonellosis. For your Red Eared Sliders, you must change their water on a frequent basis even if it does not appear to be dirty. The tank must be kept clean by sticking to a cleaning schedule that is regular. Additionally, your hands and arms must be scrubbed clean both before and after you touch the turtle.

Many turtles that are in captive do suffer from the condition called Soft Shell and this can be a very serious issue for them. This condition is caused by a deficiency in calcium as well a a lack of sunlight and vitamin D3. Symptoms of Soft Shell include a flexibility and softness of the edges of the turtle's shell. Because younger turtle's shells are usually soft, this condition may be a little more difficult to diagnose. However, if there is some form of discoloration of the shell; wherein it is turning to a color that is bleached white, then this may be an indication of Soft Shell. For this condition to be avoided or cured at an early stage you have to ensure that your turtle is getting the right amount of full-spectrum light as well as sufficient calcium in his diet. It is advised that you buy calcium powder and mix it into their food once per week.

The needs of the Box turtles are quite distinctive, and as such, you have to thoroughly research their health requirements so that you can have a healthy and successful Box Turtle ownership for many years. They too are prone to Soft Shell and Salmonellosis but these can be avoided once the proper precautions are taken. Their habitat has to always be clean as bacteria will grow in an enclosure that is unclean making your Box Turtle vulnerable to a number of health issues.

You should not handle your Western Painted Turtle unnecessarily and when you have to do so, you will need to wear latex gloves. Your hands should also be properly washed after handling the turtle so that there is a prevention of the spread of infectious diseases such as salmonella. If your Western Painted Turtle is healthy he will have healthy skin, clear eyes, clear nose and mouth, he will be active and alert, will eat regularly and his body will be rounded and his shell will be hard.

However, there are some common red flags that will be an indication of health issues. These symptoms include Abnormal feces or urine, vomiting, discharge in nose or mouth, decreased appetite, lethargy and soft shell. When their tank is over-crowded this can be a major factor with respect to them contracting diseases. As such, it is very important that the tank or pond not be overcrowded so that the turtle can remain healthy.

Map Turtles should not be handled regularly either. They need very clean water and low traffic in their living quarters to remain healthy. You should always wash your hands before and after touching the turtle so as to prevent the spreading of salmonella. Once they are healthy they will have shell that are hard and devoid of lesions, will eat regularly, be alert and active, their eyes will be bright and clear, and their nose and vent will be clear. The common health issues of Map Turtles include fungus, respiratory disease, shell rot or ulcers and swollen eyes. The fungus will manifest itself as a white fuzzy growth on his skin and shell.

You should always consult the exotic animal vet if your turtle is having issues with any of these but there are things that you will be required to do as well. If your turtle has fungus, you should ensure that their water is clean and add aquatic salt. If he presents with respiratory issues he will have a runny nose and labored breathing. You will need to ensure that his habitat is warm enough.

If your Map turtle has lesions on his shell then he more likely than not has shell rot or ulcers. If he does, then it will be necessary for you to clean his living space on a daily basis, change his diet and with the instructions of the vet, give him antibiotics. A deficiency of vitamin A or an infection is usually the cause of their swollen eyes. They should be given vitamin supplements.

CHAPTER 6- WHICH OTHER PETS TO PUT IN WITH YOUR TURTLE : FISH AND TURTLE ARE THEY A GOOD COMBINATION

The fact is that some turtles will eat almost anything you put into their tanks with them, there are just certain animals that will not work well in the same habitat as your turtle, but there are some that will make a good companion for your turtle. The feeder fish, another turtle of the same species, and turtles of another species seem to be the best choice of companion for your turtle.

However, the fish is by far the most commonly added creature to a turtle tank or pond. They fit in perfectly as they do not need any more water than is already in the turtle's habitat and they are very economical to purchase as well as to take care of.

In choosing the fish to put with your turtle, you need to find a fish that is larger than him. You should place the fish in the tank of pond then watch to see what type of reaction the turtle will have to it.

If there is no reaction, then that is usually an indication that they will be able to live together peaceably. However, if the turtle nips at the fish and bothers it repeatedly, then you may need to remove the fish from the tank. However, there is usually a very good relationship between the feeder fish and the turtle and so they would be a great choice for your turtle.

Chapter 7- Breeding Your Turtle: How To Find The Right Mate And The Process

Turtles are not very easy to breed but if you are willing to be patient and do the work that is necessary to get the baby turtles that you want, then it can be done. There are some specific steps that you should take in order to breed your turtle. Firstly you need to winterize the turtles as most turtles are not going to be breeding until fall.

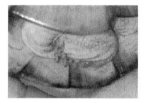

As such, it is essential that you an atmosphere that is natural as possible be created so that it mimics the ideal seasons in which they would usually experience if they were in the wild. The experts will recommend that your turtles be winterize in January and February. You winterize them by changing the temperature in their living environment to between fifty and sixty degrees for approximately six weeks and then change back to their usual temperature gradually.

Secondly, you should provide an area for them to nest. The best environment for breeding is an outdoor environment that is natural. If the indoor environment is appropriate however, it can work successfully as well. For your indoor breeding environment, you should use a box that is big enough to hold between fourteen and eighteen inches of soil as well as a comfortably hold the two turtles. You should place either sand or moss at the bottom of the box and spray the area intermittently in order to keep the area damp.

Thirdly, when they eggs have been lain after a successful mating session, they should be removed from the area. The female will usually lays between two and twelve eggs. The tops of the eggs should be marked lightly with a marker that is non-toxic. The eggs should then be carefully transported in their original position, (with the marked area of the egg always facing up) to another box that will act as their means of incubation.

The next step is to incubate the eggs with vermiculate. You can purchase a container of vermiculate at your local pet store and follow their mixing instructions. As soon as the vermiculate has been set the eggs should be gently placed in it, then the box should be sealed, leaving out a few openings for ventilation.

The temperature in the box should be kept to approximately eighty degrees. Lastly, you should leave the eggs alone and wait for them to hatch. The process should take between eighty and one hundred and fifty days.

CHAPTER 8- TIPS TO TURTLE OWNERS

It is very important for you to be certain of the environment you will be able to provide for your turtle before you make the decision to purchase one. Red Eared Sliders, Box Turtles, Painted Turtles, Map Turtles and Mud Turtles make great pets, but it is imperative that as the owner you learn about what they need to live in captivity so that you can have a successful pet/owner relationship. Turtles usually live for a very long time so you also need to be prepared to give them the care they will need for the long haul.

Male turtles are highly recommended as pets due to their size. For instance, a female Red eared Slider can grow to as big a one foot long. Smaller turtles are usually easier to manage and female turtles usually need extra special care to ensure that they remain healthy.

It is also useful for owners to know that turtles do not make the best pets for younger children. This is so because of the specialized care that exotic animals need, plus the fact that they do not enjoy being handled and touched. In addition, they often time carry infectious diseases and children under the age of five years old are susceptible bacterial illnesses. However, they still can make great family pets once the adults in the house are the ones that will be in charge of their primary care and all the interactions between the children and the turtle are closely supervised by the adults.

About The Author

Donald Wilson loves all aquatic animals, but reptiles are his favorite. He however has a special love for turtles because they are exotic animals. He grew up as an only child but he never craved another sibling due to the fact that he always had animals around him.

He always wanted a turtle but his parents decided that they were much too busy to spend the time that was needed to care for a turtle, and he was too young at one point, and then way too busy himself with both school and athletics by the time he got to the age where he was old enough to look after one.

As such, it was not until he was out of college and settled in his career that he decided to get not one, but two turtles; a Red eared Slider and a Painted Turtle.

He knows all there is to know about turtles and enjoys sharing his vast knowledge about them with all those who are interested in learning about these exotic creatures just for their general knowledge but also those who are considering them as pets. He sees his turtles as his lifetime friends as they are among the longest living creatures in existence and although they do take a lot of care, it is completely worth it to him.

Printed in Great Britain
by Amazon